cale.

I week

LAUGH with CHIRP

ha! ha!
ha!

To my grandson Gavin and granddaughter Rose with love.
  - Bob

About the illustrator: Bob Kain brings Chirp to life in every issue of Chirp Magazine. His career has included running an animation studio for 30 years, creating newspaper comic strips, and teaching cartooning to kids. Bob's most enthusiastic students these days are his grandchildren.

© 2005 Bayard Canada Books Inc.

Editor: Mary Beth Leatherdale
Designer: Claudia Dávila

Publisher: Jennifer Canham
Production Manager: Lesley Zimic

Special thanks to Hilary Bain, Katherine Dearlove, Jackie Farquhar, Angela Keenlyside, and Barb Kelly.

Chirp is a registered trademark of Bayard Presse Canada Inc.

We gratefully acknowledge the financial support of the Government of Canada through the Book Publishing Industry Development Program (BPIDP) for our publishing activities.

Library and Archives Canada Cataloguing in Publication

Kain, Bob, 1932-
Laugh with Chirp / Bob Kain.

ISBN 2-89579-071-X

1. Wit and humor, Juvenile. 2. Riddles, Juvenile.
3. Tongue twisters. I. Title.

PN6371.5.K33 2005   j818'.602   C2005-903929-9

Printed in Canada

Owlkids Publishing
49 Front Street East, Suite 200
Toronto, Ontario M5E 1B3
Ph: 416-340-2700
Fax: 416-340-9769

From the publisher of

chirp chickaDEE OWL

Visit us online!
www.owlkids.com

LAUGH with CHIRP

ha! ha! ha!

Jokes, Riddles, Tongue Twisters, and more!

Bob Kain

Owl kids

Why do birds fly south
for the winter?

It's easier than walking.

What has four
wheels and roars
down the road?

A tiger on
a skateboard.

Why do dogs bury bones in the dirt?

Because it's too hard to bury them in the sidewalk!

KNOCK, KNOCK!

Who's there?

Turnip.

Turnip who?

Turnip the music, I can't hear it.

Say this 5 times fast:

Super
summer
sandcastles

What's a bee's favourite game?

Hive-and-seek.

What do you call a polar bear in a jungle?

Lost.

KNOCK, KNOCK!

Who's there?

Lettuce.

Lettuce who?

Lettuce in,
it's cold outside.

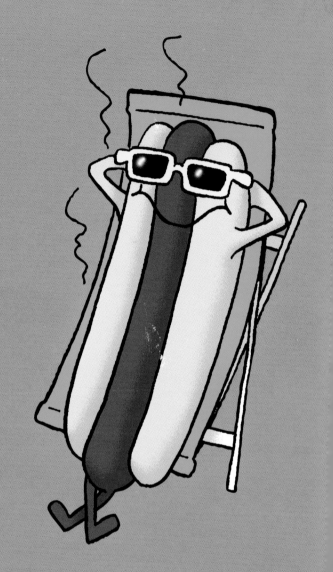

What stays hot in
the refrigerator?

A hot dog.

Say this 5 times fast:

Cute, cuddly kittens

What do you call a fairy
who doesn't take a bath?
Stinkerbell.

What has four wheels
and flies?
A garbage truck.

What kind of mistakes
do ghosts make?
Boo-boos.

Why are fish so smart?
**Because they
live in schools.**

What did the egg
say to the clown?
You crack me up.

What's black and white
and read all over?
A newspaper.

Where do snowmen
keep their money?
In a snowbank.

How do you
catch a squirrel?
**Climb up a tree
and act like a nut.**

When do astronauts eat?

Launch-time!

What do clouds
wear in their hair?

Rainbows.

What song do jaguars sing
during the holidays?

JUNGLE BELLS,
JUNGLE BELLS.

What comes from
the freezer and rings?

An ice cream phone.

How do you get
a mouse to fly?

Buy it an
airplane ticket.

KNOCK, KNOCK!

Who's there?

Comb.

Comb who?

Comb over and play.

Say this
5 times fast:

Dessert in the desert

What do
baby cats wear?

Dia-purrs!

What's worse
than having a snake
in your sleeping bag?

**Having two snakes
in your sleeping bag.**

Why don't mountains get cold in winter?

They wear snowcaps.

What keeps falling down but never gets hurt?

Snow.

Say this 5 times fast:

Monkeys munch melons

KNOCK, KNOCK!

Who's there?

Art.

Art who?

Art you going to paint me a picture?

23

Say this
5 times fast:

chirp's
cool
cape

KNOCK, KNOCK!

Who's there?

Water.

Water who?

Water you reading?

What has a
head and a tail
but no body?

A coin.

How do seals say goodbye?

Seal you later!